RADICAL INNER PEACE

EXPANDING INNER PEACE
WITHOUT MEDITATION

Desirée Sher

Editor: Tia Ross, tiarosseditor.com
Interior Design: Agata Rodriguez, agatarodriguez.com

Publisher: Desirée Sher
Vancouver, Canada
connect@desireesher.com

Radical Inner Peace - Desirée Sher. —1st ed.

ISBN 9780-9936355-1-9

OTHER TITLES BY THE AUTHOR

Refuse to Sink:
Truths for Tough Times

The Book of Affirmations for
Your Mind, Body and Soul
Volumes 1-2

The Ultimate Guide to Planning Your
Side Hustle in a Weekend

MY BONUS GIFTS TO YOU

*Bonus materials to support you on your path
to inner peace are available for download at
DesireeSher.com/bookbonus*

CONTENTS

To all the healers and coaches who showed me the way back home to my true self: I am in deep gratitude for the lessons shared.

Desirée
xo

"Go inwards. Find your inner space, and suddenly, you will find an explosion of light, of beauty, of ecstasy – as if suddenly thousands of roses have blossomed within you and you are full of their fragrance."

Osho

INTRODUCTION

My search for inner peace began more than two decades ago in a doctor's office.

I was twenty-nine years old when I asked my family doctor when I would experience inner peace. I was deeply discouraged at her response that she had patients twice as old as me asking her the same question. I was left to believe that feeling peace and happiness was reserved for monks who dedicated themselves to meditation on faraway mountaintops.

I carried on, trying unsuccessfully to make peace with the discontentment and uneasiness I felt deep in my soul. It would be another decade before I would immerse myself in a quest to find inner peace. It was not a journey I went on willingly.

It took a series of rapid-fire storms—the loss of an important relationship, a financial shakedown, and the tragic loss of my mom—before I began my quest.

While my mom's death catapulted me on a spiritual journey with a heart full of questions, my unearthing of the truth of how to create a peaceful life came only after I hit rock bottom—not once, but many times. Through a dispiriting divorce, a serious illness, multiple losses of loved ones, a betrayal, and a car accident, I was left battered, broken and desperately searching for an anchor.

My journey to find inner peace and joy took me through two dozen different healing practices and modalities. I experimented with cognitive behavioral therapy, spiritual prayer counseling, emotional freedom techniques, kundalini yoga, sound healing, craniosacral therapy, chanting, reiki, and meditation. By dedicating myself to a daily meditation practise, I began to understand the lessons I had read in hundreds of self-help books and heard about for years from the healers and gurus I sought for guidance on my journey to inner peace.

Peace and happiness are not external pursuits but internal discoveries. It was a "light bulb moment" when I realized I didn't have to chase peace. I just had to turn inward, where it had been waiting for me.

It is not by accident that you have found yourself with this book in hand, reading these words. Your soul has led you here, whispering to you that there is more for you than this pressurized, disconnected life you are living.

Living a peaceful life is a choice you make for yourself. It won't be an easy path at first to slow down, but it is possible. I know this because I made the transformation using meditation and each of the practises in this book.

While I am incredibly passionate about meditation, not everyone is ready to meditate. It takes courage to sit silently and open to the beauty and the pain of the universe. For those who want peace but don't want to meditate, I wrote this book for you!

Although this book has space dedicated to how to meditate and how to incorporate a practise easily into your life, I am not here to convert you. Instead I offer a buffet of mindfulness practices for you to choose from to expand your feelings of inner peace. You have the power to transform your external chaos into calm, joy, and beauty with or without meditation. Let's begin!

THE LIES

AND THE TRUTH

That unsettled feeling you have been experiencing that has brought you here is your soul calling to you to wake up and create a new world for yourself.

You are not alone in your anxiety and overwhelm.

The demands of modern life have left many of us feeling stressed, discouraged, and deeply tired. But you don't have to live that way. This book will light a different path for you, helping you experience inner peace no matter what is happening in your external world. However, a commitment to inner peace requires a personal revolution to slow down in a fast-moving world!

This simple suggestion of slowing down may sound radical when you have spent years striving, pushing, achieving, and running hard toward achieving success and happiness to experience equanimity.

––––––––––––––––

We are all worried we aren't doing enough.

We are worried we'll be left behind at work.

We worry about having enough money.

We worry about our health and our kids' health.

We worry about the environment.

————————————————

The list goes on. And with all this worry comes anxiousness, fear, and overwhelm.

There is another way to live.

We have been conditioned to believe that we must work more, buy more, have more, accomplish more, and THEN we will feel happiness and contentment. Despite such cultural and social misconceptions, I have discovered the opposite to be true.

I have witnessed, both personally and in my coaching practice, how slowing down and reconnecting with your soul self is the key to creating a life filled with peace and happiness.

When you put down the badge of busyness (and stop glorifying the hustle), you discover that life gets easier, struggles fade, and you feel inspired, energized, and more creative. Life gets richer when we give ourselves space to JUST BE.

The time has come to get off auto-pilot and take responsibility for creating a life that feels good from the inside out. Are you ready to say yes to radical inner peace?

MY STORY

I suffered a stroke at the age of 48. I had no risk factors that would make me a candidate for a stroke. When I recovered after two years of rehab I remained haunted about why I had the stroke. While the doctors chalked it up to just "one of those things," when I took inventory of how I ended up waking up in a stroke ward in my forties, it all made sense. I had lived in a state of stress, chaos, and overwhelm for decades.

In my external pursuit of peace and happiness, I had worked too many hours, gave up too many nights of sleep to meet too many deadlines, took on too many responsibilities, and neglected my own body to the point where my soul literally gave out. I was forced to live a different way.

There had been whispers from my body long before the stroke that I needed to slow down a decade earlier. But I equated being busy to being successful and valued. I pushed forward, ignoring the signs to slow down. Then the stroke appeared and my life turned on a dime.

When you have sacrificed yourself to the point where your soul would rather leave your body than hang around, you wake up and take notice!

The journey I invite you on starts by slowing down, turning inward, and deepening the connection to your own soul. This is where your true power lies in bringing what you desire to life. It's not an easy shift to make, but through simple practises (some that take only a minute) you can expand the peace and happiness in your life.

"Listen to your own voice, your own soul.
Too many people listen to the noise of
the world, instead of themselves."

Leon Brown

DAILY

SOUL CHECK-IN

Your first thought when you feel anxious, overwhelmed, or discouraged isn't typically 'How is my soul today?' However, when we check-in with our inner world and take time to hear the response, we can create a more peaceful and joyful life with greater ease.

Take a few moments to sit quietly now. Close your eyes. Put your left hand over your heart and ask, "What does my soul need today?"

Stay quiet and allow your soul to answer. Your soul wants to be heard. Connecting to your inner world is a sacred act and the key to creating a beautiful and peaceful life.

If you're feeling discontentment despite having attained everything you believed would bring you happiness you may be relying on external factors to bring you joy. This can leave you dependent on other people and circumstances to stay feeling happy. Yet nothing is constant in life. People come and go. Events happen. Circumstances change.

When you are focused on the external world for your emotional well-being, when life shifts your happiness and inner peace shift with it. When you anchor to the sacred space within you, you will discover peace and joy that is constant and accessible in any moment, no matter what circumstances you find yourself in.

With slowing down your life and balancing the busyness with stillness and practices that connect you to your soul, you will rediscover calm.

As you journey back to your soul, you might begin to question how you have been defi ning success for yourself. As you connect deeper to your soul, you may discover that success to you is different than you have been living.

"If you cannot find peace within yourself, you will never find it anywhere else."

Marvin Gaye

YOUR
SOUL SELF

Your soul is that loving, joyful, wise, powerful, creative, and sacred part of you that lives deep within your heart.

It is that spark of happiness that ignites within when you are connected to your purpose.

It is that surge of energy you feel when you are doing the things you love the most.

It is the gentle whisper within that pushes you to dream bigger. It is the force that pulls you forward with inspiration and guidance when you want to quit. It is your super power to create your dreams.

It is peace.

It is joy.

It is LOVE.

MEDITATION

AS A PRACTISE

My belief in the transformative power of creating a peaceful life from the inside out is why I am so passionate about meditation. And while it is not the only way to expand your feelings of calm and clarity, it is, in my experience, the most powerful. However, if it's not for you, skip ahead to learn other practises for expanding inner peace.

Meditation is for anyone who wants to bring more peace, happiness, and well-being into their lives. Meditation will nourish you and move you into the deep space of peace while simultaneously bringing you more clarity, energy, and improved health.

I love how meditation connects me to my soul-self and the sacred space within where there is no fear— just peace, joy, and love. Meditation truly saved me, pulling me back from the darkest times in my life.

The great thing about meditation is that you don't need any special tools to access its transformative powers. It's free and completely portable, fitting in perfectly to the demands of a fast-paced modern life.

Choose from dozens of styles of meditations. You can practise mindfulness or mantra meditations, breath awareness, visualizations, chanting, body scan—the list is truly endless. I encourage you to explore various styles until you find one that you connect with.

Regardless of which type of meditation you choose, the most important thing is that you meditate. Only through a regular daily practise can you access the benefits of meditation and expand your sense of peace, which will help you cope with the pressures of modern living.

Going within to find peace sounds too simple, so I think it's why we reject it in the pursuit of external pleasures.

Yet, to find peace, all you need to do is to slow down, get quiet, and connect to the sacred space within. It is the one thing in my life that I have to come to know for certain is true.

Having a regular meditation practise, no matter which style you start with, will give you the strength and the tools you need to cope with the increasing pressures of life.

"Meditation is not a way of making your mind quiet. It's a way of entering into the quiet thats already there."

Deepak Chopra

JUST BEGIN

To begin meditating, don't get caught up in the details. You don't need anything fancy. You can meditate on the floor, in a chair, or on a meditation cushion. Find a comfortable spot where you won't be disturbed. Set a timer for two minutes and then put your phone on airplane mode to ensure you won't be disturbed.

Sit tall with your feet flat on the floor or crossed on a cushion. You can keep your palms open on your thighs or in your lap.

Close your eyes; if you prefer to keep them open, begin by softly focusing on an object like a candle flame, a photo of a loved one, or a spot on the wall.

Now turn your attention inward by focusing on your breath. Inhale and exhale. Notice the air flowing in and out of your body. That's it.

Your mind is going to wander when you stop moving. That's perfectly normal and expected. The goal of meditation isn't to stop your mind from thinking, but to instead notice where your thoughts wander off. Come back to noticing your breath flowing in and out. Use it as an anchor to quiet your thoughts. In choosing what you focus your attention on you are taking back control of your mind; with it, you are showing your nervous system that there is another place to live beside chaos and overwhelm.

SETTING YOURSELF
UP FOR SUCCESS

These habits I share from my decade-long practise will support you in succeeding at meditation.

SCHEDULE IT

Claim the space for meditation by writing it in your calendar and setting a timer on your phone. I found it helpful to post a note that says *"Meditate before you operate"* on my bathroom mirror and computer as a reminder to go within first—then work.

CONNECT WITH ANOTHER HABIT

Attaching your meditation to a habit that is already a part of your daily routine will increase the likelihood you will do it. Try meditating after you brush your teeth or while the coffee is brewing.

MORNINGS ARE PERFECT

It's easy to say you will meditate later. If you leave it to later in the day you'll probably find a dozen excuses why you can't get it done. Meditating first thing in the morning increases the likelihood you'll accomplish it and creates a peaceful state of being that will accompany you throughout your day.

BRAIN DUMP

If you are worried you won't be able to settle your mind, try writing down all the things you need to do or are worried about on a piece of paper before you sit down to meditate. Not only will this calm your mind, you will also be less worried about forgetting things that bubble up when you are meditating.

START SMALL

Start small by aiming to meditate for just two minutes a day for seven days in a row. If it feels good, increase it the next week by another two minutes and do that for a week. Start small for success. No one gets off the couch and runs a marathon. They first start by getting off the couch, then going for a walk or short run around the block. Look at meditation in the same way. You are training your mind. Increase it a little every day; in no time at all you will be meditating ten minutes a day and reaping all the benefits that come with a regular practise.

Each time you mediate it will be different. Sometimes you will meditate and quickly connect to feelings of peace. It will feel blissful and that will inspire you to keep going. Other times when you sit, your experience may feel like work or it may bring up forgotten memories or challenging emotions. This is all part of the practise. Whatever you are experiencing, trust it will pass. Keep sitting!

The more you meditate, the more those feelings of peace and contentment will continue with you long after the meditation is over. It is in the moments when you feel less reactive and more loving and compassionate in circumstances that usually trigger you that you realize the practise is working to change you. It is from this soul space of centeredness and calm you empower yourself to create the life you desire.

Meditating takes practise. On the days you feel it didn't go well, or the days you miss a session, just begin again.

Meditation brings moments of bliss and peace; with constant practise it truly becomes a way of life. But it's not the only path to peace. There are other simple practices you can use to shift your stress and chaos to calm.

"The life of inner peace, being harmonious and without stress is the easiest type of existence."

Norman Vincent Peal

INNER PEACE

PRACTICES

In this little book are twenty-five practices that will realign you to that peaceful place within you. You are not creating anything new. The peace you seek has always been within you—just waiting for you to tap into it.

You might feel foolish trying these practices, perhaps even selfish taking time away from your family or business, to care for your own needs. I have found this to be true for many of my coaching clients, especially moms.

It was incredibly hard for me to slow down when I first started to meditate and make these peace practices part of my daily life. Yet, waking up in the stroke ward was a powerful reminder that if I didn't manage my stress, my daughter could lose her only parent. I urge you not to let yourself get so depleted that you get sick or your body cries 'enough' with an illness or, as in my case, a stroke.

When we are connected to that peaceful place within, we have the resiliency and strength to meet the demands of life. Yet, when life speeds up we tend to forgo the self-care. That's why I call on you to start a personal revolution in your own life where the practices that release your stress and realign you to the sacred peaceful space within become your daily non-negotiable rituals.

The following techniques aren't all or nothing practices. Try some things. Go slow. Repeat the practices that feel good for you. You will know when you have found the practices that work for you by tuning in to how you feel.

Please make a promise to yourself now to take care of your soul and don't break that commitment to yourself. You, sweet soul, are deserving of a beautiful life filled with peace, fulfillment, and joy!

1. BASK IN
SILENCE & SOLITUDE

Each day, make a little time to be alone in silence and solitude. Time spent in solitude gives your soul the opportunity to catch up with your body. It also allows your body and mind to rest and reset.

In our modern society it can be hard to find a quiet place. Solitude doesn't have to be sitting alone for hours. Alone time can be found in small moments scattered throughout your day. Try leaving the radio off in the car when you drive to work, going for a walk without your phone, or finding a quiet spot to rest during your lunch break.

It is in the quiet you hear the voice of your soul. You will hear it through wisdom, creative inspiration, and guidance. You may experience this as a gut feeling or in a dream. Stay open to listening to your soul's whispers throughout your day. The quiet will allow you to re-energize and realign to peace in a noisy world.

2. PRAYER

Prayer is a path to connect to a Higher Source. You may call that source God, Spirit, Love, Universal Energy, or something else. You do not need a set of religious beliefs or affi liation to prayer. Prayer is about opening your heart and deepening your connection to the Divine spirit.

If you've never prayed I invite you to start by getting quiet and bringing your awareness to your heart. Can you take a few breaths in and out of your heart space? Start by giving thanks for all that is good and abundant in your life. Feel the connection to your heart deepen with gratitude. (Gratitude is a powerful practise to joy.) Then speak the truth from your heart, requesting any assistance you need in this moment. "I am stuck and need guidance on my next steps." "I feel alone and long for connection." "I am struggling today; help me." Ask for what you need.

Let your words transform into feeling. It is in that depending connection and intimacy you find peace.

3. SET AN INTENTION
FOR YOUR DAY

Setting a daily intention helps you bring your heart and mind into alignment with what you desire in your life. I love setting an intention right after I take a few deep breaths. When you identify how you want to be in the world today, you are setting an intention of how you're going to move through your day. Whenever you find yourself out of alignment with this intention, repeating it out loud or silently to yourself will anchor you back to your desire. Here are some intentions I have used that may inspire you.

I am peace

Breathe

Lead with love

Courage over fear

All is good

4. CONSCIOUS
BREATH PRACTISE

It may seem silly to talk about breathing. We do it without thinking, so why would we need to practise it? In this busy, fast-moving life, most of us are breathing in a rapid shallow manner. And in times of stress we may even be holding our breath without noticing it. This causes us to deprive our entire body and brain from full oxygenation. And we can't be our best when we aren't fully oxygenated!

When you find yourself stressing out or moving into overwhelm, bring your attention to your breath. This will send a signal to your brain and your nervous system that it's safe to relax and reminds your nervous system that there is another place to live than in overwhelm and chaos. It's very simple. (You may want to close your eyes for this practise.)

· Take a deep breath in through your nose.

· Fill your lungs and become aware of them expanding fully. Then slowly exhale completely.

· Repeat five times until you feel yourself aligning back to peace.

From this place of calm you can move forward with your day with clarity and confidence.

5. POSITIVE

AFFIRMATIONS

When life gets stressful it's easy for our thoughts to send us down a negative spiral. Affirmations are simple but powerful statements that we say to ourselves to change our thinking. When you use them repeatedly, affirmations can help reprogram the unconscious beliefs that we carry about ourselves. They have been instrumental for me in moving through my own limiting beliefs and reclaiming peace.

Start with two words: I AM.

What you place after them will help shape your reality. Ask yourself how you need to be to create the life you desire. It all begins with what you believe about yourself. Here are a few affirmations that I've used.

I am confident and capable.

I am a powerful creator of my dreams.

I am resilient and get through my challenges with case.

Repeat the affirmation both silently and out loud, really owning the words with passion and energy. You may want to post the affirmation where you can see it as a constant reminder of what you want to become. You can post your affirmation on your bathroom mirror, on the fridge, in the car, or on your phone. Please be patient with yourself. Just because you use an affirmation doesn't mean you will overnight create a new world. It took years of experiences for you to build the limiting beliefs. Transforming your mindset takes time, but affirmations work if you keep an open heart and mind.

Check out the book's bonuses
for affirmations
you can download.

6. APPRECIATE

NATURE

Spending time in nature will instantly connect you to your soul and the sacred peace within. Even if you can't get into the forest, when you wake up spend a few minutes looking up at the sky and breathing in some fresh air. Stepping outdoors on your lunch break and letting the wind blow, the sun shine, or the rain and snow fall on your face will also do wonders for restoring your sense of peace.

The next time you head outdoors you can ritualize your experience by intentionally connecting to the sacred space within. Ask a question that you have been seeking an answer to or ask what it is you need to know right now.

As you walk or sit in the silence, nature will provide you with the answers and insights you seek.

Being in nature regularly can transform your life. Feeling the wind or smelling the earthy pine or salty ocean air can calm your mind and open your heart, helping you to expand your feelings of peace.

7. SACRED
WATER PRACTISE

One of the easiest ways to connect to the sacred peaceful space within is to take a bath. Bathing instantly removes you from all distractions, calms your mind, and slows your breathing. Add some Epsom or Himalayan bath salts and essential oils to the water. Light candles. Play some relaxing music (making sure your phone is safely away from the water), and you'll nourish your soul on many levels. As you drain the tub, imagine everything that is blocking your peace going down the drain with the water. If you only have a shower, visualize the water flowing over you and washing away everything that feels heavy and constricting. You'll honestly feel lighter when you step out after this water practise.

8. UNPLUG

Being connected to our phones twenty-four hours a day, every day, can add to feelings of stress and overwhelm. We have so much information coming at us that it's impossible for our brains to keep up. Consider taking a break from your phone for a few hours (phone-free mornings) or a full weekend where you unplug. Notice how you feel when you disconnect once the initial anxiety of being offline passes.

9. GROUNDING

Take off your shoes and socks and stand supported by the earth. Even a couple of minutes with your bare feet soaking up the earth's energy on grass, dirt, sand, or snow will discharge stress and reestablish the connection to your soul and the inner peace within.

10. FEED YOUR
SOUL WITH MUSIC

Music can have a tremendous effect on how we experience our day. Music has the power to uplift, bringing peace and happiness to any moment. Explore different kinds of music and make a playlist that you can listen to when you need more peace. Check out the book bonuses for playlists to soothe your soul.

11. CHANT
YOUR OWN NAME

Chanting creates energy of joy, peace, and purposefulness that will empower you throughout your day. While there are many mantras you can use for this practise, I have discovered chanting your own name is powerful. It creates an immediate connection to your soul. (The first time I chanted my name I cried.) To hear yourself sing your own name will help you align you to your sacred self and you'll feel an incredible amount of love for yourself.

12. SIMPLIFY

It's hard to slow down when you're doing a million things at once. While you may pride yourself on multi-tasking, a conscious decision to do less allows you to place more focus on what's most important to you and do it better. Start your day by asking yourself what is one thing I can do today to make me feel successful? Focus on getting that done first and you'll feel pleased with yourself at the end of your day even if all the other tasks go undone.

This is the revolution! If you want more peace you're going to have to make some changes. Adding less to today's to-do list may not be easy, but with time you'll feel less anxiety and have more compassion for yourself when things remain undone. There is always tomorrow.

13. JOURNALING

Journaling is a powerful tool to reduce stress, gain clarity on a challenge, expand creativity, and increase your self-awareness. You don't need to commit to journaling every day. It's a practise you can come back to whenever you need to unwind. There are many different ways to journal.

· You can free write for a set time. If you're new to journaling, set a timer for 10 minutes and let your pen flow over the page. Just write whatever your heart wants to express. Don't judge it or edit what you write. Let your pen move across the page, margin to margin, until the timer goes. When you're finished, review what you wrote for any surprise insights or messages from your heart.

· You can write down a daily list of things you are grateful for in a gratitude journal. When you focus on all the abundance in your life, you will instantly feel uplifted. I started this practise a decade ago and it keeps me grateful for all the things in life.

· Use a meditation journal to capture your experiences, observations, or wisdom gained through your practise. It's fun to look back and see how your self-awareness expanded with sitting.

· A self-love journal is a special book where you write down all the things you love about yourself. If the idea of this makes you say 'no way', I highly encourage you to start this type of journal. Perhaps you have lost sight of your magic? If so, it's time to grab a journal and start writing love letters to yourself.

· There are also many journals available to purchase online that have prompts if you're stuck on what to write about.

If this practise resonates with you treat yourself to a pretty notebook and pen. Leave your journal somewhere you see it every day and you'll be drawn to writing.

14. GET

CREATIVE

Your soul is a powerful creator. Tapping into the creativity that is within by expressing yourself through creating something made by your own hands will deepen your connection to your peace. While your brain might be telling you that you are not an artist, we all are. (You are a creator of your beautiful life!) When you give permission for the artist within to come out and play, your soul becomes joyful. Grab some supplies and start creating at home or explore taking an art class where you can try new mediums of artistry.

15. LIGHT

A CANDLE

Lighting a candle instantly creates reverence for your soul. Light a candle to evoke a sense of peace within your home or office. Choose a candle free of harmful chemicals.

16. THE

POWER OF SMELL

By choosing a scent that promotes relaxation and encourages spiritual openness, you can expand your inner peace.

I like to use essential oils during meditation in two ways. The first is by diffusing the oil into the air using a diffuser. The second is by applying essential oils to my skin. You can also apply a few drops to your palms, rub your hands together, and then bring them up to your nose and inhale.

Two oils I use regularly are lavender for its calming properties and eucalyptus to help clear my airways so I can bring my breath deeper into my body.

I also keep a rose water atomizer in my living room and office. A quick spray has numerous benefits, including soothing and calming your mind.

17. ACTIVE
GRATITUDE

Try focusing each day on what you have in your life, instead of what is missing, and you will open yourself to more joy. Writing down what you are thankful for in a journal is a powerful exercise, but at times when we are overwhelmed that activity can feel like too much.

Active gratitude is a simple practice I often do while driving. I invite you to think of three things you are grateful for in this moment. It can be as simple as "I'm thankful for this delicious coffee," "I am thankful for the people in my life who love me," "I am excited for the long weekend ahead," or "I love the song on the radio." Speaking them out loud creates a vibration that hits your soul. You'll feel yourself smile with joy when you do this practise. And when you feel happiness you will feel more peaceful.

18. OPEN YOUR EYES
TO BEAUTY ALL AROUND

Make time to pause and awaken to the beauty that is all around you. By appreciating the little pleasures in life we bring our focus back into the present moment where peace is found. Little things like the smell of coffee in the morning, the sound of your child's laugh, the scent of spring flowers, or a walk on the beach can fill your heart with gratitude for this amazing life. When we keep our eyes and heart open to beauty we truly find it everywhere.

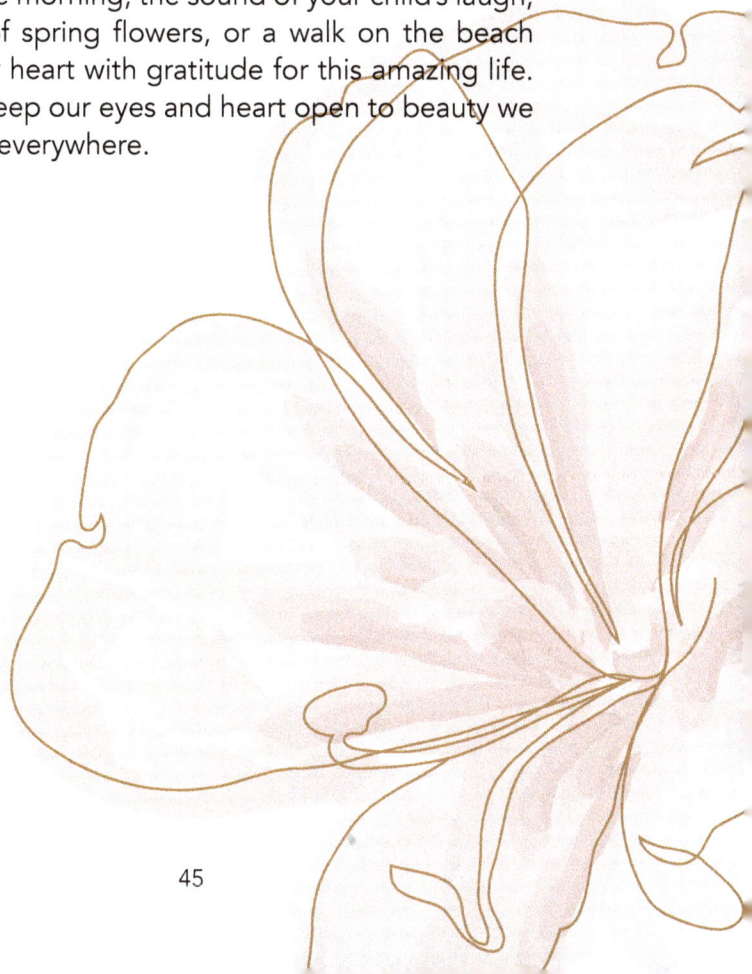

19. COURAGE
TO SAY NO

When you are overwhelmed or feeling depleted, it's impossible to refuel your soul if you continue to sacrifice your own needs for everyone else's. Learning to set boundaries isn't always easy, but it is vital for your inner peace.

When you say "no" to others, you are saying yes to your sacred self. And when you say "yes" to yourself, it opens you up for more opportunities and abundance in every part of your life. If something doesn't feel good or robs you of your inner peace, it's not worth it

Saying "yes" to yourself will get easier with practise. You don't have to go into lengthy explanations when your family, friends, or co-workers ask you to take on another task. Simply say, "It's just not possible for me to do that."

When you say no to the things that don't feel good, you create more space in your life for the people, activities, and things that make your soul happy. And you deserve to be happy!

"Underneath the chaos of everyday living, peace is patiently awaiting our discovery... go within."

Jaeda DeWalt

20. THE

POWER OF SLEEP

Do not underestimate the power of sleep. Very few of us get enough sleep in this modern life. A lack of sleep is a huge cause of stress. Aiming for at least seven hours a night is best to let your body, mind, and spirit rest. That might seem a huge leap in your busy life so why not try to embrace naps? They aren't just for babies! Taking a short nap while your child sleeps or a ten-minute break at your desk or in the sunshine will revitalize your soul with renewed energy. If you want to feel less stress, increasing your sleep is a great place to start.

21. ALTERNATE
NOSTRIL BREATHING

When you feel overwhelmed or anxious, try this simple technique of alternate nostril breathing to relax your busy mind and body and return back to peace.

Raise your right hand to your face and place your first two fingers between your eyebrows. Rest your right thumb lightly on your right nostril. With your pinkie and ring finger resting gently on your left nostril, breathe in deeply through your nose.

Then, close your right nostril with your thumb as you exhale through your left nostril.

Breathe in through the left nostril; as you pause, close the left nostril with your pinkie and ring finger. Release the thumb on the right nostril and breathe out through the right nostril.

Inhale through the right nostril, close with the thumb, release the fingers from the left side and exhale through the left nostril.

Try performing this for 5-7 cycles.

Breathe out. Breathe in. Switch sides.

22. CONNECT
WITH YOUR PASSIONS

Making time each day to do something you are passionate about or that brings you genuine pleasure is vital for living a happy life. Too many of us have replaced our passions with duties and obligations. Most people have decided they don't have time to explore their heart's pleasures and passions in this modern life and end up starving their souls of joy.

Think of three things you'd love to do that would bring you more joy. Say them to yourself. Even if you can't commit to them today, whenever you feel overwhelmed and want more peace, repeating those three words will bring yourself a little joy and peace. Sometimes three little things can make a big impact.

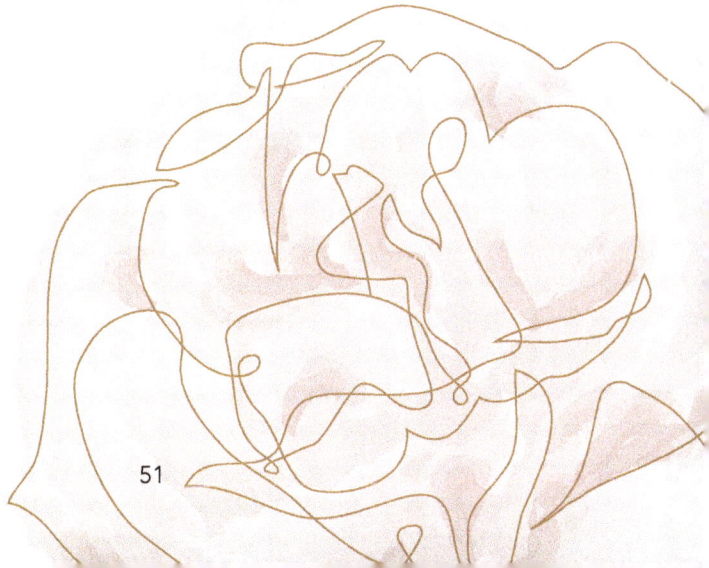

23. UNCHAIN

YOUR HEART

Is there a hurt from your past that you can't let go of? Maybe it's playing on repeat, occupying space in your mind and consuming your energy?

When we have been hurt or betrayed, it can be hard to forgive the one that hurt us and move forward with living our best life. However, replaying past hurts only fuels bitterness and resentment, which robs us of the peace and joy we deserve.

One practise that is incredibly powerful in transforming pain into peace is the ancient Hawaiian prayer for forgiveness known as Ho'oponopono. The philosophy behind this practice is that we are each responsible for our reality—the good and the bad. And, we each have the power to transform our reality with forgiveness and love.

This isn't a practise for the person who hurt you. It's about giving yourself the permission to forgive and let go of past hurts and trauma, freeing your mind and your heart to reclaim joy, peace and love again.

The *Ho'oponopono* prayer is simple but powerful.

> I am sorry.
>
> Please forgive me.
>
> Thank you.
>
> I love you.

Repeat as often as needed and watch miracles unfold.

24. A PEACE
SYMBOL

Having a sacred reminder that you can carry to align yourself back to your sacred peaceful sanctuary within whenever you feel overwhelmed or out of balance is a beautiful gift to give yourself. Your symbol could be anything that the act of looking at or touching it brings you back to the sacred space: a crystal, a feather, a rock, seashell, or anything else that resonates with you.

25. CREATE A SACRED SPACE
IN YOUR HOME OR OFFICE

Creating a sacred space within your home or office will support your practices and reinforce your intention to invite more peace into your life. It doesn't have to be complicated or costly. Start by adding small items that are special to you to a shelf or table—a scented candle, fresh flowers, a rock, seashell, crystal, or a photo of a loved one—anything that sparks joy and love in your soul. You may want to add a small rug to mark the space, a soft pillow, or a luxurious scarf to keep you warm. Make your space so beautiful that you want to sit there to meditate, write in your journal, or just spend time near it.

"It isnt enough to talk about peace. One must believe in it. And it isnt enough to believe in it. One must work at it."

Eleanor Roosevelt

MAKE SOUL TIME

If you feel selfish taking time away from your family to engage in meditation or other sacred practices, remember you cannot give to others when you are empty within. I urge you to schedule time each day to nourish your soul by connecting to your inner world. Consider this book your permission slip to put yourself first, to nourish yourself with love and gentleness. You are worthy of your own love and attention. And if you struggle to give yourself permission I am giving it to you now!

Try starting your day with new practices that promote inner peace instead of reaching for your phone and jumping straight into email or checking your social media accounts. A few ideas to incorporate sacredness and peace into a morning ritual could include:

· Setting an intention of how you want to feel in your day before you get out of bed

· Taking three deep belly breaths before you get out of bed

· Reading an inspirational book

· Saying a prayer or blessing

· Telling one person in your life you love them

· Honouring your body with some form of gentle movement

· Starting your day by giving thanks to be alive

· Journaling

· Simply listening to your favourite music over a cup of tea for a few minutes before tuning into the outside world

· Commit to a routine that leaves you feeling grounded and calm and ready to handle anything that comes your way.

RESISTANCE

When it comes to meditation or trying one of these new inner peace practices, you may feel resistance. Resistance is fear. It is that internal block you experience when you think about doing something new but then don't do it.

Our inner critic often surfaces whenever we start a new habit. It can sabotage our best efforts with stories about why we can't do something, including meditation. Some common stories that may surface for you are:

"I am too busy."
"It feels selfish."
"I feel fine today, so I'll start tomorrow."
"This won't help me."

We all have stories and limiting beliefs that hold us back from taking action on bringing our heart's desires to life. We often don't start on a new path because our heads are filled with thoughts telling us why we've left it too late, it will be too hard, and nothing will change. Fear will prevent you from taking those first few scary steps every new journey begins with.

Yet, when you push forward from your comfort zone, despite the resistance you feel, you grow, and what once seemed impossible feels possible.

If you want to go a little deeper, try this exercise to shift from fear into action.

First, open your mind to the belief that a change in your life can bring you the peace you long for. It is all waiting for you on the other side of fear.

Next, acknowledge that you feel resistance. Fighting your resistance will only give it more power over you.

Sink into the feeling. Where it is located? Do you feel it in your throat? Your chest? Your stomach? Someplace else?

Let yourself feel what arises. Don't try to change it. Allow the feelings to come. Trust that the intensity will fade. It will. You will be okay. Keep breathing deeply and let the feeling come and then go.

When the feelings have subsided, ask yourself, "What am I afraid of?" Identifying the block will allow you to start moving past them.

Capture any insights and guidance in a journal or on your phone. Then take action anyway! The quickest way to overcome resistance is to take that first step in a new direction. What is one action step you can take toward creating more of the peace you desire in your life today?

FREQUENTLY
ASKED QUESTIONS

How can I meditate or do these practices when I don't have time?

We don't have time. WE MAKE TIME. I invite you to pause all the doing. Take a moment for yourself because when something is important to us, we find the time. Remember your motivation and why you wanted to start in the first place. Are there tasks you can eliminate or chores you can delegate to your partner or kids to make more time? Look for energy leaks in your life (social media is a big one) and I'll guarantee you will find five minutes each day to meditate—*if* peace matters to you.

What should I do when I keep falling asleep while meditating?

You are probably tired, so honour that with a nap. In our modern life, many of us are living in sleep-deprived states. Let yourself rest. If falling asleep with every meditation continues, try taking small breaks or vary the time you meditate. You can also try meditating with your eyes open. Try softening your gaze and focusing in on an object like a flickering candle.

How do I stop thinking during meditation?

Meditation is not about emptying your mind or stopping your thoughts. It's about becoming aware of your thoughts and then practicing refocusing your attention.

What can I do when I am too restless to sit?

Try sitting and observing the restlessness without any reaction. Notice it but continue to sit. This trains the mind and gives you back the control. Or you can try taking your meditation outdoors with some movement like a mindful walking meditation. Or let go of meditation for now, and try one of the other practices in this book to expand feelings of peace.

What should I do when uncomfortable feelings come up?

Stay with the thoughts or emotions that arise. Our natural tendency is to avoid the uncomfortable feelings like anger, sadness, or anxiety. But feelings are powerful messages from our soul. Be curious about what comes up and let yourself feel it. The only way these feelings will end is if you let yourself experience them.

Am I doing it right?

Yes! If you are meditating, you are doing it perfectly right for you! Please don't get caught up in the how-to; just do it. We all worry that we are doing it wrong when we start anything new. You might even worry you look funny and are doing it wrong. You aren't! There is no perfect way. Celebrate your efforts. You're doing it, and that's what matters.

FINAL

THOUGHTS

It takes courage to slow down and claim more for yourself in our high-pressured society. I applaud you for taking the first step with the purchase and reading of my book. My hope is that you are guided back home to your soul for an expanded sense of peace, contentment, and joy.

I encourage you to try meditation and the other practices I shared to connect with your peaceful space within. You can't change your life if you only read. You need to take action.

Embarking on a journey of transformation is not always easy. There will be days you want to quit; I urge you to keep going. It won't be long until you look back at your old life and give thanks that you found your way home to your true self.

If you let the light of peace and love enter your heart through the path of your soul, you will open your life up to miracles and magic. You have just one life on this planet. It's time to transform it into the peaceful and happy life that it was meant to be.

With big LOVE for you!

ACKNOWLEDGEMENTS

Writing a book does not happen alone and my book was no different.

This book would not have come to life without the constant encouragement and support of my daughter Maya. I am forever grateful for you supporting my vision when I first shared my idea and uplifting me when I became discouraged.

Thank you to my writing coaches Alexandra Franzen and Lindsey Smith who showed me that even a small book can carry a big message. I am grateful for all your support on my journey to put this book into the world.

ARE YOU LIVING A

LIFE ALIGNED WITH YOUR SOUL?

Take the Quiz

DesireeSher.com/quiz

ABOUT

THE AUTHOR

Desirée is a mindset coach and international speaker from Vancouver, Canada.

Drawing on her own experience as a reformed Type A entrepreneur and busy mom she works to promote a more peaceful world by sharing her wake-up call to live life in a radical more peaceful way.

Desirée has shared her message of inner peace, resiliency and passion with thousands around the world on international stages, on social media, and as the past host of the Power up with Desiree Show on Conscious Talk Radio. She believes that connecting to the peaceful place within is the first step in creating a life you love.

CONNECT WITH THE AUTHOR

DesireeSher.com

www.ingramcontent.com/pod-product-compliance
Lightning Source LLC
Chambersburg PA
CBHW041826090426
42811CB00010B/1118